T0279641

IMAGES
of America

THE BELGRADE
LAKES REGION

IMAGES

of America

THE BELGRADE LAKES REGION

Eric Hooglund

ARCADIA
PUBLISHING

Published by Arcadia Publishing
Charleston, South Carolina

Printed in the United States of America

Library of Congress Control Number: 2022951595

For all general information, please contact Arcadia Publishing:
Telephone 843-853-2070
Fax 843-853-0044
E-mail sales@arcadiapublishing.com
For customer service and orders:
Toll-Free 1-888-313-2665

Visit us on the Internet at www.arcadiapublishing.com

To the memory of my maternal aunt Janet George (1925–2019), who introduced me, my younger brother, and our 14 maternal cousins, as well as all our children and grandchildren, to the Belgrade Lakes, and to the memories of Lawrence Sturtevant (1917–1999) and Carol Nye (1919–2010), who collected hundreds of old photographs and documents to begin preserving the history of Belgrade and the Belgrade Lakes region.

CONTENTS

ACKNOWLEDGMENTS

The Belgrade Historical Society (BHS) is a nonprofit organization staffed by an all-volunteer board of directors, similar to other historical societies in Maine and other states. My role as a board member has been to edit our newsletter and to accession donations, responsibilities that have provided me the opportunity to acquire a constantly deepening knowledge of the unique, interlinked history of the Town of Belgrade and the wider Belgrade Lakes region. Thus, when Arcadia Publishing approached the BHS about the prospect of producing a book about the region for its Images of America series, I realized that, with more than 300 black and white photographs in our collection pertaining to the period 1890 to 1950, this could be a feasible and interesting project.

Although I selected the photographs and composed the captions for this book, many people helped me in diverse ways, and I deeply appreciate their advice and assistance. Among my fellow BHS executive board members, I thank Dianne Dowd, BHS president; Duane Farnham; Loyce Hayslett; Rod Johnson; Adelaide LaLime; Robert and Sandra Lewis; Don and Nancy Mairs; and Doris Mathias. Among my Belgrade and Rome friends, I thank Polly Beatie; Peg Churchill of Bear Spring Camp; Pam Cobb of Camp Runoia; Elizabeth and Fred Fontaine; Kyle Hochmeyer, who patiently instructed me in the art of scanning photographs in accordance with Arcadia specifications; Carol Johnson, president of the Belgrade Lakes Association; Judith Johnson of Friends of the Belgrade Public Library; Craig Killingbeck for expert help with photographs; Beverley Megill; Richard Nye of Loon Lodge; Marie and Bill Pulsifer; Marcel Schnee; Ben Swan of Pine Island Camp; and the late Daniel "Tree" Robins.

INTRODUCTION

The Belgrade Lakes region in central Maine has been an important summer tourist destination since the 1870s. It is comprised of a chain of seven separate lakes connected by streams southeast of the Kennebec Highlands. Their collective name comes from the town of Belgrade, which received its charter in 1796. John Davis, the son of a settler family, suggested the name based on his travels to Europe in 1789–1791, where he witnessed celebrations to mark the liberation of the central European city of Belgrade (in modern Serbia) from two centuries of Muslim Turkish rule.

About 80 years after Belgrade's founding, the first "tourists" discovered that the seven lakes were ideal for fishing. In the late 19th century, tourists came to these lakes via trains from major cities to Belgrade's two railroad stations: One on the southwest and the other on the northwest shores of Lake Messalonskee. Upon arrival, tourists—initially single males but, by the late 1890s, entire families—hired horse-drawn carriages for transport to reservations at lodges on one of the lakes. By 1900, "the Belgrade Lakes" had become—and remains—the collective name for the seven lakes, although each one, locally called "ponds," has its own distinct name.

The most easterly lake, East Pond, covers 1,813 acres (2.8 square miles). Its southern third is in the town of Oakland (in Kennebec County), while its northern two-thirds are in Smithfield (in Somerset County). A wetland, the East Pond Bog, extends from its northwestern shore, through which meanders a 2.5-mile stream, the Serpentine, which flows into North Pond at Smithfield village. North Pond's entire eastern shore is within Smithfield, but its northwestern shore is within Mercer (also in Somerset County), while its southwestern shore, including the virtually closed-off inlet known as Little Pond, is in the Kennebec County town of Rome. At approximately the midpoint of North Pond's southern shore, and right at the Rome and Smithfield boundary, the Great Meadows Stream meanders for some two miles before merging into Great Pond, the largest of the Belgrade Lakes. About half a mile before Great Meadows reaches Great Pond is the border of Smithfield and the town of Belgrade. Thus, the final half-mile of Great Meadows Stream is shared between Rome and Belgrade, as is the northwestern shore of Great Pond. Nevertheless, most of the lake's 8,239 acres (about 13 square miles) are within Belgrade's borders.

In addition to North Pond, two smaller lakes also drain into Great Pond: McGrath Pond (486 acres) and Salmon Lake (526 acres). Both are in North Belgrade and their waters form part of Belgrade's eastern boundary with Oakland. Geologically, these ponds are not two separate bodies of water but a continuous one with a very constricted "waist," where land formations force McGrath's water into a narrow channel for approximately 250 feet before the water broadens out again into Salmon Lake. Near the southeastern end of Salmon is a stream that flows west for about one mile into the southeastern part of Great Pond.

There are several islands in Great Pond; the largest, Hoyt Island, has many summer cottages along its two-mile length. Other islands include Chute, Crooked, Joyce, Oak, and Pine Islands. There are many tree-covered peninsulas, locally called "points," along which are sited youth camps, private camps, and year-round homes. About midway down the western shore of Great

Pond, Mill Stream exits the lake and meanders for about two miles to drop over a natural eight-foot cascade into Long Pond, at the village of Belgrade Lakes. Long Pond extends over 2,500 acres (3.9 square miles) and is 31 miles long. Large boulders and an island constrict it to a narrow passage at Castle Island, effectively dividing the lake into Upper Long Pond and Lower Long Pond. The entire eastern shore of Long Pond is within Belgrade, but the northern and western shores of Upper Long Pond are within Rome, while the western shore of Lower Long Pond is within the town of Mount Vernon.

At its southern end, Lower Long Pond tapers into Belgrade Stream, which meanders south into Mt. Vernon, then east and south again back into Belgrade, then northeast where it merges into the marsh area of Lake Messalonskee at Belgrade Depot. Messalonskee is the second largest of the lakes in the Belgrade chain, extending over 3,510 acres (8 square miles) and is nine miles long. It is the only lake that has a Native American name: Messalonskee is a Wabanaki term for "white clay." No archeological evidence has been found that Native Americans ever lived on Messalonskee or the other lakes, but they did fish and hunt among the lakes, which were near their villages along the Kennebec River, into which the lakes drain.

Belgrade and Sidney share the southern two thirds of Messalonskee Lake, although in Sidney it commonly is called Snow Pond, after Phillip Snow, an 18th-century settler of that town who briefly had a summer fishing and hunting cabin on the Belgrade side of the lake (around 1774–1776). The northern third of the lake is in Oakland, where Messalonskee Stream exits the lake and drops over a high cascade (waterfall) and then meanders northeast for about two miles, then turns southeast and meanders through the city of Waterville for three miles, finally merging into the Kennebec River south of the downtown. For over 100 years, Messalonskee Stream was used for industrial purposes and became of the most polluted waterways in the state. Since the early 2000s, cleanup efforts and the construction of bike and walking trails have helped to restore much of the stream's pre-industrial qualities, and fish have even returned.

One

FARMS AND MILLS

This c. 1865 photograph shows Rev. Joseph Cummings (1834–1912), farmer and respected Baptist minister, in front of his house on the Manchester/Readfield Road (Route 135) north of Belgrade Depot. He is standing between his son John M. Cummings (1859–1945) and the family's horse. The Cummings farm was typical of several large and productive ones in the Belgrade Lakes region in the post–Civil War era, with apples being an important cash crop. Although the front porch of this house was enclosed in the 20th century, its exterior remains largely unchanged today. (Sturtevant Collection, BHS.)

This is a late 1880s drawing of the Stevens farm, also on Manchester Road, built between 1800 and 1850. After the Civil War, the Stevens farm was notable for its diverse fruit and nut trees. The house still stands, but with its 20th-century additions and modifications, looks very different. (Sturtevant Collection, BHS.)

Greenlief Stevens (1831–1918) was a Civil War hero. The Stevens Knoll Monument at Gettysburg National Cemetery commemorates his victory there. After the war, he became a lawyer and left the family farm to practice law in the state capital of Augusta, about 15 miles south. (Sturtevant Collection, BHS.)

Simeon and Thankful Wyman, with their six children, were the first family to settle in Belgrade, in 1774. They built this brick house on Belgrade Hill overlooking Lake Messalonskee for their son James and his bride in about 1799. Town meetings often convened here prior to 1815. After James's grandson died without heirs in the early 1900s, the town sold the house. (Old House Survey, BHS.)

Belgrade's Town Meeting House was built in 1814. Annual town meetings were convened here every March from 1815 to 1872. After serving as a quarantine place for a smallpox patient in the summer of 1872, men were afraid to hold the March 1873 town meeting here, and it moved to the new Masonic Temple in Belgrade Depot. Subsequently, the cemetery used the old meeting house to store its records and equipment. (BHS.)

John Rockwood built this farmhouse in 1800 on what now is Route 135 in Belgrade. A barn on the left burned in the late 19th century, while a two-story addition on the right was demolished around 1930. Rockwood heirs sold the house in the 1950s. As of 2020, the original large fireplace for cooking and heating, and several original wide floorboards, were still intact. (Old House Survey, BHS.)

The Rockwood family donated land for the construction of Belgrade's first church in 1826–1828. Reverend Cummings often preached here in the late 19th and early 20th centuries. Originally known as the South Church, it has continued to serve as a house of worship and community social center for over 190 years. Since the mid-20th century, locals have called it the Old South Church. (Carol Nye Collection, BHS.)

The Minot House, near the Rockwood House and the Old South Church, has sections from both the early and late 19th centuries. John Clair Minot (1872–1941) was raised here and collected the family histories of the first settlers in Belgrade from his grandfather and John Rockwood to write the history of Belgrade chapter for *Illustrated History of Kennebec County, Maine, 1799–1892*. (Sturtevant Collection, BHS.)

This is a c. 1910 photograph of John Clair Minot. He moved to Boston in the early 1890s and eventually became editor of *Youth's Companion* and an editor at the *Boston Herald* newspaper. (Sturtevant Collection, BHS.)

Blanche Minot drew this early 20th-century pencil drawing of the Minot farm. She was the younger sister of John Clair Minot and, like her brother, moved to the Boston area, where she attended teacher's college and art school. (Sturtevant Collection, BHS.)

Seen here is a c. 1905 image of Blanche Minot. She was an artist noted for her watercolor paintings, a few of which are in the BHS collection. Her studio was attached to her home in Waverly, Massachusetts, but, like her brother, she often returned to the Minot farm in summers and for Christmas. (Sturtevant Collection, BHS.)

Paul Yeaton (1803–1893), a successful farmer and skilled wood craftsman, built this stately house on Belgrade's West Road in 1826. Successive Yeaton generations continued to live in the house for over 150 years. More recently, new owners have operated the house as a bed-and-breakfast inn. (Old House Survey, BHS.)

This earliest-known photograph (taken around 1865) of Belgrade Lakes village looks north. Its location on a narrow peninsula between the Mill Stream outlet from Great Pond and Long Pond had insufficient land for farms, but a natural eight-foot waterfall where Mill Stream flows into Long Pond spurred the development of diverse mills beginning in 1797, and later stores and taverns. (Sturtevant Collection, BHS.)

John Chandler built the first store, gristmill, and sawmill near the dam on Mill Stream in Belgrade Mills and then constructed this large house in 1831 for a home and tavern, as the main stagecoach road from Augusta to Farmington passed through the village in the early 19th century. The pillars and second-story verandah are 20th-century additions. (Old House Survey, BHS.)

John Chandler built this store in 1838 in Belgrade Mills with granite quarried from Vienna Mountain. He paid two Irish masons 50¢ per day and all the rum they could drink to haul the granite slabs across frozen Long Pond in the winter of 1838. In 1927, Charles Brown converted the store into a home by having a stone mason cut more windows into the building. (Markowitz Collection, BHS.)

This iconic house with the widow's watch cupola on its roof was built in 1843 in Belgrade Mills to serve both as a family residence and a tavern for passengers traveling by horse and stagecoach on the main road between Augusta (20 miles south) and Farmington (20 miles northwest) in the mid-19th century. Since 1918, it mostly has been an inn under various owners. (Old House Survey, BHS.)

In 1849, the railroad arrived in Belgrade, connecting it to Portland in the south and Waterville to the east. The town had two stations: Belgrade Depot (shown in this 1890s photograph) near Belgrade Stream, where it merges into the southwestern shore of Messalonskee Lake, and North Belgrade on the lake's northern shore. (Merrow Collection, BHS.)

The North Belgrade train station on Messalonskee Lake is seen here in the 1890s. On the left is the water tower used to fill the tanks of steam locomotives. (Merrow Collection, BHS.)

In 1857, Joseph Taylor built this stone house with rocks and pebbles he collected on his farm over a 25-year period. His horses transported his corn to a canning factory in Belgrade Depot and barrels of his apples to the North Belgrade train station for shipping to urban markets. Taylor's stone house still stands on Oakland Road in North Belgrade. (Carol Nye Collection, BHS.).

In 1872, general store and spool factory owner David Golder led a fundraising effort to build the Union (Methodist) Church in Belgrade Lakes. Although initially open only from late spring to early fall, during renovations in the 1920s and 1930s, heating equipment enabled the church to become an important year-round civic and social, as well as religious, center. (Sturtevant Collection, BHS.)

This one-room District 11 grammar school in Belgrade Lakes village opened around 1889. As the new millennium was approaching in 1899, it acquired the name New Century School. After a larger two-room school was built in 1929, the town sold New Century School to the newly formed local chapter of the American Legion. (Pope Collection, BHS.)

This is Belgrade's first public high school in Belgrade Depot. It opened in 1904 and graduated its first class in 1908. It moved to the second floor of the new Central School in 1924, and the old high school subsequently became a private home. (Lewis Collection, BHS.)

The Foster barn, completed in 1888–1889, features a special natural cooling design to prevent stored hay from catching fire in hot summers. The barn remains unaltered and has been listed in the National Register of Historic Places. (Old House Survey, BHS.)

Watson Farm in North Belgrade is pictured here in the 1890s. LuBertha Watson is seated at center, with her father, Andrew (left), and her mother (right). LuBertha became a teacher and later married Will Withers, who made wooden barrels and boxes that Belgrade farmers used for storing and transporting their apples. (Martha Withers Pink Collection, BHS.)

This c. 1902 photograph shows teacher LuBertha Watson with her students in front of the one-room district grammar school on Horse Point Road in North Belgrade. (Martha Withers Pink Collection, BHS.)

The Alexander family farm in North Belgrade, across the road from McGrath Pond Road, is pictured in the 1890s. The house burned in the mid-20th century. The Alexander farm property extended to McGrawth Pond, and at the beginning of the 20th century, the family built several small cabins on the lakeshore to rent to summer tourists. The Alexander Camps also provided meals, and most guests returned for several successive summers. (Merrow Collection, BHS.)

The Mills farm on Belgrade Hill is pictured around 1890. The farm produced diverse crops, including apples and corn. In 1920, the house and barn burned to the ground. (Mills Collection, BHS.)

The Mills farm is pictured here during winter in the 1890s. The Mills men are preparing the horses and wooden rollers to roll (or pack down) the snow to make winter roads passable before the invention of snowplows. (Mills Collection, BHS.)

This c. 1900 photograph of the Mills farm shows men loading barrels of apples onto a wooden "train" for horses to pull to the North Belgrade train station, where they would reload the barrels onto rail cars. (Mills Collection, BHS.)

By the early 20th century, Belgrade farms collectively were producing about 6,000 bushels of apples, mostly for export via train all over the eastern seaboard. In this c. 1902 photograph, wooden barrel maker Will Withers is loading apple storage barrels at his North Belgrade factory near the Salmon Lake dam. Early tourism and prosperous agriculture were becoming intertwined. (Martha Withers Pink Collection, BHS.)

In 1882, the Cascade Woolen Mill opened in Oakland next to the dam on Messalonskee Stream, the outlet for the entire Belgrade Lakes watershed. Here, the stream drops over a natural 100-foot cascade, and the abundant waterpower spurred Oakland's development as a small industrial center in the late 19th century. The mills provided employment for many men from Belgrade, Rome, Sidney, and Smithfield. (Pope Collection, BHS.)

Two

Early Tourism

A mail boat arrives at Jamaica Point Camps on Great Pond in Rome in 1905. The annually increasing number of private cottages and summer camps on Great Pond prompted the Belgrade Lakes Post Office to start a summer mail boat service in 1900, which has continued for over 120 summers. Summer resident and playwright Ernest Thompson featured the mail boat in his 1978 play *On Golden Pond* and in the 1981 movie version for which he won an Academy Award for best adapted screenplay. (Sturtevant Collection, BHS.).

In the summer of 1874, Charles and Abby Lord Austin opened their home in Belgrade Lakes as the Central House, providing beds and meals for men from urban areas coming to fish in the lakes. This is generally considered the beginning of tourism in the Belgrade Lakes region. (Sturtevant Collection, BHS.)

By 1880, the Austins had built Liar's Paradise with two upper floors of bedrooms to accommodate the ever-increasing number of tourists. The first floor was a social hall, where men gathered in the evenings to tell stories about the giant fish that got away. Charles Austin is seated second from right. (Sturtevant Collection, BHS.)

In the 1890s, the Austins built this four-story addition to the Central House. It included a large—and popular—dining room in the rear overlooking Long Pond. (Sturtevant Collection, BHS.)

In 1880, the Seventh Day Adventist Church established the first summer campground on Lake Messalonskee, a short walk south of the North Belgrade train station. Beginning in 1896, more substantial cottages gradually replaced the original tents and simple cabins. Adventists continue to gather at Lakeside for religion and recreation during August. (Lewis Collection, BHS.)

This 1890s photograph shows a family on the porch of the Birches, one of the large cabins at Hillside Camps on Great Pond in Rome. By the 1890s, middle-class urban men wanting a summer fishing vacation were bringing along their families. (Sturtevant Collection, BHS.)

This late 1890s photograph shows the Hillside Camps beach area on Great Pond. Swimming for sport was not yet popular, but bathing in the lakes was. Men and women bathed at separate times, and it was considered improper to be present when the opposite gender was bathing. (Pope Collection, BHS.)

In 1900, North Belgrade resident Alpheus Spaulding opened the Salmon Lake House on Richardson Pond, which he renamed Salmon Lake. The guest house provided meals, rooms, and a beach for tourist families. This c. 1902 image shows guests relaxing on the front porch and lawn. (Mills Collection, BHS.)

This 1907 photograph shows Salmon Lake House guests aboard Spaulding's horse-drawn passenger carriage ready to be transported to the nearby North Belgrade train station, five miles away, after a relaxing week on the lake. (Mills Collection, BHS.)

This is an early 1900s photograph of the Salmon Lake House in winter. There were no tourists in the winter—just a quiet home for the Spaulding family. (Mills Collection, BHS.)

The first summer youth camp for boys, Camp Merryweather, opened in 1900 on Great Pond's northeastern shore, North Belgrade, as only the third youth camp in the nation. This photograph shows founder Henry "Skipper" Richards (with hat) sitting with camp counselors. Henry's wife, Laura (daughter of Julia Ward Howe, author of the "Battle Hymn of the Republic,") helped manage the camp. (Sturtevant Collection, BHS.)

In 1902, Clarence Colby, at center in the second row, established Pine Island camp for boys on Pine Island in southeast Great Pond, southwest of Camp Merryweather. Colby envisioned summer camp as an education: Boys would learn useful skills by living in a rugged but cooperative outdoor environment, an experience to prepare them as adults to contribute to society in diverse and useful ways. (Swan Pine Island Collection, BHS.)

In the late 19th and early 20th centuries, guides—boat-owning young men who were experienced fishermen—had an essential role in the development of the lakes' tourism, as few city-raised, middle-class men knew how to fish or row a boat. This 1905 photograph is of Edwin Megill, a guide from New Jersey who eventually settled in Belgrade Lakes. (Carol Johnson Collection, BHS.)

In the years 1895–1905, as many as 74 guides typically were based on Mill Stream behind Belgrade Lakes village. The stream provided guides with ready access to both Great and Long Ponds. This c. 1905 photograph is of Capt. Bert Curtis, the first guide to operate a steamboat, which could accommodate at least a dozen passengers. (Carol Nye Collection, BHS.)

This photograph from the early 1900s shows Thomas Golder, brother of general store owner Henry Golder, on the left, in the boat yard he established on the Belgrade side of Mill Stream. It was the first boatyard, and guides brought their boats here for repairs. Golder's house is in the background on the Rome side of the stream. (Carol Nye Collection, BHS.)

Henry Golder bought the first automobile in Belgrade. In this faded 1905 photograph, he is driving a Stanley Steamer; his wife is sitting with him in front on the left, while her cousin Ida Chandler sits in the rear. Note that the steering wheel is on the right. (Carol Nye Collection, BHS.)

Millard Gleason is pictured on the family farm in North Belgrade. He opened Snug Harbor on the southeast shore of Great Pond in 1903 and built a central dining room and social hall plus several guest cottages. As an adult, author E.B. White (1899–1985) wrote an essay about his first visit (in 1905) to Snug Harbor with his parents and siblings as a young boy. (Gleason Collection, BHS.)

Snug Harbor's waterfront and docks on the Great Pond are pictured here, which E.B. White referred to as Gleason's Shore in his essay. This photograph shows Belgrade guide Ernest Merrow (1876–1961) rowing his self-made boat to the dock. Snug Harbor cabins are visible on the shore behind him. (Gleason Collection, BHS.)

This c. 1905 image of Snug Harbor's main building shows guests arriving from or departing for the North Belgrade train station via Gleason's horse-drawn carriage, probably the same one that met E.B. White's family on his first visit as a child. The station was about six miles east of Snug Harbor. (Gleason Collection, BHS.)

The Snug Harbor dining room is seen here in 1905, where E.B. White would have eaten meals during the two weeks in August he spent at Snug Harbor with his family. (Gleason Collection, BHS.)

This is an 1894 image of tourist tents on North Pond in Smithfield. Note that the tents seem to be on raised wooden platforms, which was common at sport/tourist camps in the late 19th and early 20th centuries. Permanent cabins with beds, as well as other furniture such as chairs and dressers, began replacing tents after 1900. (Merrow Collection, BHS.)

This 1894 photograph shows unidentified women tourists exploring the shore of North Pond. While some women enjoyed accompanying their husbands when the latter hired guide boats to take them out into the lakes, most preferred to stay on land while the men were fishing. (Merrow Collection, BHS.)

This c. 1900 image shows guests relaxing on the porch of the North Pond House, an early and popular tourist inn in Smithfield. Its success prompted the owners to add numerous cabins between 1902 and 1913. These were popular among families with children. Guests in the cabins ate their meals at the main house, and also went there to socialize. (Merrow Collection, BHS.)

Three

GOLDEN AGE OF TOURISM

In 1900, Charles Hill of Waterville opened the luxurious Belgrade Hotel on Long Pond in Belgrade Lakes. Each of its initial 50 rooms had a private bath. A live orchestra serenaded guests in the evenings as they dined on multi-course meals in the large, ornate dining room. Other amenities included electricity throughout the hotel, a nine-hole golf course, tennis courts, a sunken garden, a supervised school/activity room for children of hotel guests (many of whom spent several summer weeks at the hotel), wooded walking trails, and a private beach on Long Pond. This image was captured in 1910 after two new wings, including the one on the left with two turreted towers, had been constructed, adding a total of 52 more rooms over 10 years. (Sturtevant Collection, BHS.)

Charles Hill (1852–1931) is pictured around 1905. After the 1899 purchase of the extensive forested tract of land along Long Pond upon which he intended to create the Belgrade, Hill successfully lobbied town officials and the US Post Office over two years to change the village's name from Belgrade Mills to Belgrade Lakes. (Sturtevant Collection, BHS.)

The Belgrade Hotel's lobby is seen here as it appeared in the promotional brochure for 1910. The lobby appears to be comfortably furnished to the standards expected by its primary clients: bankers and industrialists from New York and other large cities who met here both to conduct business and socialize. (LaLime Collection, BHS.)

This c. 1907 photograph shows the Belgrade's horse and carriage that transported guests to and from the Belgrade Depot train station, six miles south via the West Road. By 1911, a six-passenger Stanley Steamer automobile had replaced the horse and carriage. (Carol Nye Collection, BHS.)

After years of lobbying, Hill finally persuaded Western Union to open a telegraph office in the Belgrade in 1910. Pictured is Alta Poland, the hotel's telegraph operator for five seasons. She met Gould Rogers, the station master at Belgrade Depot, and they married in 1914. (Pope Collection, BHS.)

The Belgrade's guests included wealthy entertainment, financial, and political personalities of the early 20th century. This photograph shows the private cottage where famous Broadway singer Anna Held (1872–1918) stayed with her entourage when she spent several summer weeks at The Belgrade between 1908 and 1915. (Carol Nye Collection, BHS.)

The Belgrade's kitchen and dining room staff pose on the hotel's Long Pond dock in this undated photograph, probably from the early 1940s. African Americans began coming to the Belgrade Lakes region for summer jobs as early as 1912. (Liebfreid Collection, BHS.)

Main Street in Belgrade Lakes is seen here around 1905. A benefit of having the Belgrade in the village was electricity, as the new electric poles demonstrate. The store on the left was owned by Harvey Parker, son-in-law of the Austins, who owned the Central House. From 1910 to 1940, Bean's Bait and Tackle Store occupied it; the owner, Ervin Bean, was a younger brother of merchant entrepreneur L.L. Bean. (Sturtevant Collection, BHS.)

Ervin Bean, the tall man standing second from left, is seen on Main Street in the late 1930s. His bait and tackle store is the second building on the left in the background. Bean installed a marble-top soda fountain after 1920, which was popular with both local and summer children, even getting a favorable mention in an E.B. White essay. (Pulsifer Collection, BHS.)

The Central House Garage was built around 1911 to accommodate the new automobiles that guests were driving to the Belgrade Lakes region and the new taxis that were replacing horse-drawn carriages for transporting guests to and from Belgrade Depot. (Dowd Collection, BHS.)

By 1912, Wilson Clement had purchased this six-passenger Stanley Steamer to transport guests between the hotels in Belgrade Lakes and the Belgrade Depot. The driver is Charles Stuart, with station manager Gould Rogers on the left. In 1929, Stuart and his wife, Eva, became the drivers for Belgrade's school bus. (Sturtevant Collection, BHS.)

The increasing number of automobiles created a demand for better roads. This photograph from 1919 shows a state road crew constructing a newly paved road on Belgrade Hill at the junction of Routes 8 (to North Belgrade and Smithfield) and 11 (east to Oakland and Waterville). (Sturtevant Collection, BHS.)

This rare photograph of Belgrade Lakes was taken during the winter in the early 1950s. The Central House Garage was sold after a larger garage/service center was built across the street. The former garage was renovated into a recreation building with a stage for concerts, movies, and plays; it also had a bowling alley in the back. Initially called the Acme Theater, by the 1940s, its name was the Casino. (Johnson Collection, BHS.)

After the Central House Hotel was sold in 1916, the new owners updated its interior to compete with the Belgrade for middle-class patrons and changed its name to the Lakeshore Hotel. They moved Liar's Paradise to the shore of Long Pond and renovated it into the Paradise Cottage, seen in this c. 1923 photograph. (Sturtevant Collection, BHS.)

By 1924, this new three-story building (center) had replaced Liar's Paradise. Its entire ground floor was a spacious, furnished lobby, and each of the two upper floors contained six large bedrooms with full bathrooms. The intent of the lobby seems to have been to compete with the Belgrade for wealthier clientele. (Sturtevant Collection, BHS.)

This interior photograph of the Lakeshore Hotel's new lobby was taken in the late 1920s. In size, the quality of its furnishings, and its large stone fireplace, the lobby was comparable to the nearby Belgrade Hotel. Following the end of Prohibition in 1933, the Lakeshore added a cocktail lounge, and hotel guests could bring their drinks back to the lobby to enjoy. (Merrow Collection, BHS.)

This late 1920s photograph shows part of the Lakeshore Hotel's dining room. Although the original dining room was from the 1890s, it was updated with new furnishings and dinnerware. Its windows provided a view of Long Pond and a stunning view of the sun setting over the hills of Rome on the lake's western shore. (Sturtevant Collection, BHS.).

This is a late 1920s view of the Lakeshore Hotel from its docks on Long Pond. The dining room is the small one-story building on the left. The kitchen (not visible) was under the dining room. Like the Belgrade and other hotels, guests were on the "American plan"—breakfast, lunch, and dinner were included with the room. (Sturtevant Collection, BHS.)

In 1918, Ervin Bean acquired the large house with the widow's watch cupola and renovated it into the Lake View Manor, a tourist inn with a new dining room overlooking Long Pond. The dining room was not only for paying guests, but was also open to the public. (Pope Collection, BHS.)

In 1921, Guide Edwin McGill and his wife renovated their barn into a restaurant with guest rooms on the second floor and called it the Locusts' House, after two locust trees in the yard. By 1940, they had bought the house on the right and converted it into hotel-style bedrooms connected to the restaurant by the arcade at rear center. (Pope Collection, BHS.)

The construction of privately-owned camps, cottages, and summer homes in the Belgrade Lakes region outpaced new hotels and inns between 1900 and 1929. Popular illustrator Charles Gibson (1867–1944), the creator of the "Gibson Girl" images in the pre–World War I era, built Overlook, a summer mansion on Belgrade Hill overlooking Lake Messalonskee. (Old House Survey, BHS.)

In 1926, playwright Eugene O'Neill (1888–1953) rented Loon Lodge, a less-pretentious summer home on Great Pond near Belgrade Lakes. That summer, he and actress Carlotta Monterey carried on a public affair; he abandoned his family and fled to France with her. They got married in 1929 after O'Neill obtained a divorce from his wife. (BHS.)

Cosmetician Elizabeth Arden (1881–1966) opened her Maine Chance beauty spa on Long Pond in 1934. The property was located where the borders of Belgrade, Mount Vernon, and Rome meet but mostly was within the latter town. She bought several local farms to make sure her clients' meals consisted of fresh, organic products. (Pope Collection, BHS.)

Guests for the Maine Chance farm and hotels usually arrived at Belgrade Depot, seen in this photograph from the early 1940s. Chauffeurs met them at the station and drove them and their baggage to their destinations. (Sturtevant Collection, BHS.)

Guests of the Belgrade Hotel pose on its golf course in the early 1930s. The well-maintained, nine-hole course extended in front of the hotel, and guests usually sat on its 400-foot verandah to watch games. Its caddy house was located approximately where the Sunset Grill restaurant is today. (Mills Collection, BHS.)

This is a summer 1922 photograph of the first float plane in the Belgrade Lakes region landing on the Long Pond dock of the Belgrade Hotel. Its arrival was a major event at the time. Fifteen years later, the first airmail plane landed on docks farther north near the dam to deliver and pick up mail from the Belgrade Lakes post office. (Markowitz Collection, BHS.)

This 1937 aerial view shows the location of the Belgrade Hotel (center right) in relation to its golf course (center) Long Pond (upper left), Belgrade Lakes village (center to upper left), and the Mill Stream outlet from Great Pond (right). The village, within easy walking distance of the

hotel, benefitted from its presence. Hotel guests often hired guides on Mill Stream to take them on cruises and/or fishing trips in Great Pond. (Mills Collection, BHS.)

An October 1956 fire reduced the 400-foot-long, four-and-a-half-story Belgrade Hotel and all its contents to ashes. Closed for the season and its water system shut off, fire trucks from Belgrade and area towns were unable to save the famous landmark. Its destruction marked the end of an era, and it took years for Belgrade Lakes to recover. (Pulsifer Collection, BHS.)

Four

FAMILY AND
FISHING CAMPS

The first sporting camps, mostly for fishing, began operating in the Belgrade Lakes region in the late 19th century. Although initially for men, within a few years, they began bringing along their families and the sporting camps evolved into family camps that provided boats for men to go fishing with any wives and/or adolescent children who wanted to join them. Families stayed in lakeside cabins and ate meals in a central dining room. In small camps, the dining room served as a social center after meals, but larger camps tended to have separate social halls where guests could gather in the evenings or on rainy days. Many of these camps, such as Castle Island Camps on Long Pond (pictured), have been operating for over a century, often welcoming successive generations of the same families during the summers. (Old House Survey, BHS.)

This is an early 1890s photograph of Belgrade Lakes Camps on Hoyt's Island in Great Pond. "Sports" who came to fish in those years needed to hire guides, who had boats, fishing gear, and knowledge of the lakes. (Sturtevant Collection, BHS.)

Hillside Camps on Great Pond in Rome, one of the earliest sporting camps, dated to the early 1890s (see chapter two). This 1922 photograph of the new administration building shows that Hillside was keeping up with the changing times. (Sturtevant Collection, BHS.)

Another early sport camp was the North Pond House in Smithfield. As noted in chapter two, the North Pond House added several individual cabins and this central dining hall in the early 20th century. (Sturtevant Collection, BHS.)

MAIN LODGE, JAMAICA POINT CAMPS, BELGRADE LAKES, MAINE

In 1910, Jamaica Point Camps added this rather upscale new inn featuring a dining room, social hall, and private guest rooms on the upper floors for those desiring a more comfortable experience than the close-to-nature one in the cabins along Great Pond's shore. (Sturtevant Collection, BHS.)

C.B. Bridges opened the Red Oaks Lodge in 1910. It was an upscale fishing camp on Great Pond, close to its outlet stream to Long Pond. Its road approach was via Belgrade Lakes village. The lodge was destroyed in a 1929 fire, and its surviving cabins were sold. (Sturtevant Collection, BHS.)

Alden Farm Camps was established on East Pond in Oakland in 1911, and the Alden family still operates it today. Many guests return for one or two weeks every summer, and some of their adult children and grandchildren have continued the family tradition over successive generations. (Sturtevant Collection, BHS.)

This is a typical individual camp at Alden Farm. Most camps are spacious enough to accommodate large families or groups, which is one of the reasons the same guests return summer after summer. The food in the communal dining room also has a long reputation for being exceptional. (Sturtevant Collection, BHS.).

Seen here is a view of East Pond from an Alden camp. Iconic Maine white birch trees obscure Alden's expansive beach and dock area. East Pond is relatively shallow, and its temperature in the summer tends to be warmer than Great and Long Ponds. (Sturtevant Collection, BHS.)

Alden's dining room not only is popular with its guests, but also with some Belgrade, Oakland, Sidney, and Smithfield residents who can make reservations for dinners. Many friendships have developed among local patrons and the summer guests who return to Alden over several summers. (Sturtevant Collection, BHS.)

In 1911, George Mosher opened Bear Spring Camps next to the Bear Spring at the head of the Jamaica Point peninsula on Great Pond in Rome. E.B. White was one of its famous guests. Like Alden Farm Camps, it has been managed by the same family for over a century, and many of its guests are successive generations of the same family. (Sturtevant Collection, BHS.)

A typical camp at Bear Spring Camps is seen here. George Mosher's descendants have followed his friendly management style, and most recently, his granddaughter and her husband are the proprietors. Individual camps are periodically updated, and newsletters keep summer patrons informed about Great Pond in the fall, winter, and spring. (Sturtevant Collection, BHS.)

By the early 20th century, extensive sport fishing was depleting natural fish stocks in the Belgrade Lakes chain. The Belgrade Lakes Association, founded in 1908, promoted conservation and helped to persuade the State of Maine to open this fish hatchery in North Belgrade for stocking the lakes with bass, perch, salmon, and trout. (Merrow Collection, BHS.)

In 1914, A.C. Roy opened the Oakland Boat & Canoe Company in Oakland. This photograph from the 1920s shows one of his hand-crafted wooden boats on display in front of his store. The private and sport camps in the Belgrade Lakes region were major buyers of his Dolphin Craft boats between 1914 and 1940. (Patricia Roy Collection, BHS.)

In 1917, Chester Thwing opened Woodland Camps at the end of a long peninsula jutting into Great Pond with 18 cabins and a central dining hall, seen in this c. 1920 photograph. In the early years, guests could only access Woodland by boat, but eventually, a road was cut through the woods to the camps, which still exist as private condominiums. (Sturtevant Collection, BHS.)

Millard Gleason, operator of Snug Harbor (see chapter three), sold it in 1925 and opened Whisperwood Inn and Cottages on Salmon Lake in North Belgrade. Whisperwood, under successive new owners since the 1940s, still operates. (Sturtevant Collection, BHS.)

New Depot. N. Belgrade. Me.

This is a c. 1912 photograph of the new North Belgrade train station. Summer sports and tourists heading for camps on the eastern shore of Great Pond, Salmon Lake, McGrath Pond, or the northern shore of Lake Messalonskee typically arrived at this station during the early 20th century, but passenger train service was discontinued in the early 1950s. (Mills Collection, BHS.)

Pictured is a 1940s-era advertising brochure for the popular Clements Camps on the southeastern shore of East Pond in Oakland. Most guests arrived by train at the North Belgrade or Oakland train stations, where taxis met them and drove them and their baggage to the camps. (Sturtevant Collection, BHS.)

This c. 1945 photograph shows a typical cottage at Clements Camps. The cottages were comfortable, the meals in the central dining hall were satisfying, East Pond's waters were pleasantly warm for swimming, and anglers always caught fish. (Sturtevant Collection, BHS.)

Degen's Camps on Great Pond in Belgrade featured simple cottages like this one. They were affordable to rent and popular among middle- and working-class fishing enthusiasts during the post–World War II era. (Sturtevant Collection, BHS.)

Wheeler's Housekeeping Camps, located on a small peninsula, Birch Point, on the eastern shore of Salmon Lake (Oakland), is famous for its sunsets. (Sturtevant Collection, BHS.)

This early 1950s view of East Pond is from Davey's East Lake Camps, which were on the southeastern shore near Clements Camps in Oakland. Guests liked the fishing and swimming at Davey's. (Sturtevant Collection, BHS.)

This 1940s photograph of a roadside sign on Route 11 at the intersection with Route 8 on Belgrade Hill indicates directions to the numerous camps on Great Pond and Salmon Lake. It also signifies the arrival of the automobile age, which would have a devastating impact on train travel in the Belgrade Lakes region and in Maine overall. (Liebfreid Collection, BHS.)

Five

YOUTH CAMPS FOR BOYS

The Belgrade Lakes region was one of the earliest areas in the country and the first in Maine where summer youth camps for boys developed. This photograph from the mid-1940s shows a group of senior Camp Kennebec boys hauling their long canoe over rapids in the Allagash River in northern Maine. The camp's wilderness adventure was a highlight of the summer camp experience for boys who had spent several summers preparing for it. Soon, they would be going on to college or work. Camp Kennebec's wilderness adventure was legendary, even being featured in a *National Geographic* article. (Camp Kennebec Collection, BHS.)

Maine's first boys' camp, Merryweather on Great Pond, operated from 1900 to 1937, but descendants of its founders, Henry and Laura Richards, still own the property. This stone memorial topped with a lantern was erected in 1921 on the lake shore to honor 10 former campers who lost their lives in World War I; the lantern disappeared in the early 2000s, a victim of a winter storm or theft. (Merry Weather Collection, BHS.)

In 1908, Clarence Colby sold Pine Island Camp to Dr. Eugene Swan, who continued to manage it in accordance with Colby's ideals and principles. In this c. 1920 photograph, he is seated with his two sons, Ripley and Eugene Jr. (nicknamed "Jun"). (Swan Pine Island Collection, BHS.)

Dr. Swan's wife sits next to a hammock outside the family tent on Pine Island around 1912. As the camp mother for many years, many boys, especially when they were pre-teenaged, remembered her as a sympathetic listener whenever they felt pangs of homesickness. (Swan Pine Island Collection, BHS.)

On Pine Island, the boys traditionally slept in tents on wooden platforms, slightly raised above the ground. Typically, each tent contained four beds. These early 20th-century tents were gradually replaced with cabins in the late 20th century. (Swan Pine Island Collection, BHS.)

Alfred Kinsey (1894–1956) was a counselor at Pine Island in the summers and a student at Bowdoin College (1914–1917) in Maine. His early scholarly interests and research were botany and insects, not human sexual behavior—for which he became famous beginning in the 1940s. (Swan Pine Island Collection, BHS.)

Wilson Parkhill (1901–1978) was a counselor during his college years, and although city-born and raised, he loved rural Maine and Pine Island, eventually becoming its assistant director. He also bought a house in North Belgrade adjacent to Pine Island Road, where he and his wife, Margaret (1907–1983), raised their daughter, who had a long association with Pine Island's sister camp for girls, Runoia (see next chapter). (Swan Pine Island Collection, BHS.)

George Victor Hugo is pictured as a Pine Island camper in the summer of 1940. The great-great-grandson of 19th-century French author Victor Hugo, he had fled France with his family as Germany was invading and establishing the puppet Vichy regime there in the early months of World War II. (Swan Pine Island Collection, BHS.)

Dr. Swan (right) and his son Eugene Jr. (left) whom family and friends called "Jun" are pictured here. In 1947, Jun succeeded his father as Pine Island's director, and continued in that role until 2000, when his son Ben became the third generation of Swans to manage this famous boys' camp. (Swan Pine Island Collection, BHS.)

This photograph shows the interior of Pine Island's "big dorm," which was originally built by Clarence Colby in 1902. It was used for diverse purposes in the early 20th century, when the campers slept in tents. (Swan Pine Island Collection, BHS.)

Camp Kennebec, founded in 1907 by educator Louis Fleisher on the western shore of Salmon Lake in North Belgrade, operated on similar ideals and principles as those that guided Pine Island's philosophy, including having the campers sleep in tents, as seen in this photograph. (Camp Kennebec Collection, BHS.)

Developing boating and swimming skills were essential aspects of the Camp Kennebec experience. Boys who had spent four or more summers at the camp looked forward, at ages 14 to 17, to participating in the weeklong wilderness trip on northern Maine's Allagash River. (Camp Kennebec Collection, BHS.)

More than any other youth camp in the Belgrade Lakes region, Camp Kennebec had close ties with many local businesses and farms. Anderson's store/post office/gas station literally was a next-door neighbor and provided the camp with groceries and diverse other supplies, including fuel for boats, as well as weekly laundry services and, sometimes, even movies for the campers. (Sturtevant Collection, BHS.)

In the late 1920s, Kennebec opened a camp for younger boys, ages 7 to 10, on the southern shore of Salmon Lake. Affectionately known as "Kennebec Junior," the youthful campers slept in cabins while their less strenuous camping experience focused on age-appropriate fun and games, as well as learning to swim. The New England Golf and Tennis Summer Camp, a coed facility for preteen and teenaged golf and tennis enthusiasts, now occupies this site. (Camp Kennebec Collection, BHS.)

Perhaps inspired by the success of Camp Kennebec, in 1914, Edward Teller founded Camp Arcadia for boys, north of Kennebec on the western shore of Salmon Lake. The campers slept in a cluster of small cabins, each containing two to four beds, and ate their meals in this unique open-air dining porch (special screens could be unfurled for protection in rainy weather). (Sturtevant Camps Collection, BHS.)

This photograph from the early 1920s shows Camp Arcadia's social hall, a typical feature of youth camps, where campers gathered when they were not engaged in the diverse structured outdoor and water activities that occupied much of their daily schedules. (Sturtevant Camps Collection, BHS.)

Edward Teller, the founder and director of Camp Arcadia, is kneeling at center and lighting the campfire around which all the campers, counselors, and staff gathered each evening (unless it was raining). The evening campfire was a ritual at most youth camps, and at Arcadia, it included

storytelling and group singing. Most campers came from the metropolitan New York City area, and the campfire was an essential part of the overall experience that Arcadia provided. This photograph is from the early 1920s. (Sturtevant Camps Collection, BHS.)

This photograph from the early 1920s shows Camp Arcadia boys practicing boating skills with their counselors on Salmon Lake. Camp Arcadia closed at the end of the summer of 1927. A similar boys' camp, Cedar Crest, was on the Oakland shore of Salmon Lake from 1915 to 1944. (Sturtevant Camps Collection, BHS.)

Mort Eiseman opened Camp Belgrade for boys in 1937 on the former property of Jo-Lee girls' camp. Located on Great Pond, just north of Pine Island and the Snug Harbor sport camp, it was a classic boys' camp, offering swimming, basic boating skills, horse riding, and such outdoor sports as tennis and archery. This c. late 1940s photograph shows campers and their riding instructors astride horses. (Sturtevant Camps Collection, BHS.)

Here is a rare photograph of a summer camp in winter. It shows Camp Belgrade's buildings "buttoned up" for the winter and snow everywhere. The Great Pond shoreline (not shown) would have been frozen, with snow covering the ice, a sight—and site—the campers might not recognize. This image is undated but is probably from the late 1940s. (Sturtevant Camps Collection, BHS.)

In 1926, Robert Webster of Brunswick, Maine, established Wyconda, a boys' camp on the western shore of upper Long Lake, the first youth camp on this lake. This photograph from the late 1940s shows the campers practicing their boating skills. The camp's lodge is on the shore to the left. (Sturtevant Camps Collection, BHS.)

Following the examples set by Pine Island and Camp Kennebec, the boys at Wyconda slept in tents on raised wooden platforms, with two to four boys per tent. (Sturtevant Camps Collection, BHS.)

Educational tutoring was an integral part of the camp routine at Wyconda. This c. early 1940s image shows boys studying in Wyconda's comfortably furnished lodge. (Sturtevant Camps Collection, BHS.)

Six

COED AND GIRLS' YOUTH CAMPS

Camp Runoia girls row a long canoe on Great Pond in 1915. Runoia opened in 1907 on Salmon Lake, but by 1914, it had outgrown its original home. That fall, its directors bought a larger property on Great Pond at the end of Long Point (called Lord Point prior to the 1960s), a long and wide peninsula jutting out into Great Pond. Both new and returning campers helped move boats and other items from the old to the new campsite. This post-move photograph shows about 10 older girls exploring—and apparently enjoying—the much larger Great Pond environment. More than a century later, Runoia remains at its "new" site. (Cobb Runoia Collection, BHS.)

In 1905, the three Hersom sisters of Belgrade Lakes opened Camp Abena, the first overnight summer camp for girls in Maine and one of the first in the United States. This photograph shows the Abena campus on Great Pond near Belgrade Lakes village, with tents on raised platforms and the Bungalow dining hall and social hall at center in the rear. (Sturtevant Camps Collection, BHS.)

Seen here is Camp Abena's assembly building. Note the large stone chimney in the center of the left side wall. It indicates a large fireplace inside, a common feature for youth, sport, and even private camps. (Sturtevant Camps Collection, BHS.)

Pictured is the Middle Lodge on Camp Abena's campus, which may have been a dormitory for staff. After Camp Abena closed in the early 1980s, its property was sold for development, and all its buildings were demolished to make way for private homes/camps. (Sturtevant Camps Collection, BHS.)

In 1907, Jesse Pound (right) and Lucy Wiesner (left) opened Belgrade's second girls' camp, Runoia, at the Wait Hill Farm, the property of which included frontage on the southeast shore of Salmon Lake, south of the boys' Camp Kennebec, which was founded the same summer. (Cobb Runoia Collection, BHS.)

Wait Hill Farm is pictured here in 1907 before Jesse Pound and Lucy Wiesner began renovating it into the first Camp Runoia. Salmon Lake's shore is not visible from the position this photograph was taken because the lake is behind and below the small hill on which the house stands. The farm was approached via Taylor Woods Road, near the North Belgrade train station. (Cobb Runoia Collection, BHS.)

Camp Runoia girls pose for a c. 1913 group photograph at the North Belgrade train station as they wait for the train that will take them back to their hometowns after a summer at camp. (Cobb Runoia Collection, BHS.)

Runoia at Wait Hill farm had a less than ideal waterfront for swimming and boating, but it had adequate acreage for horses, and learning the art of grooming and riding horses developed as a major activity, one that has continued to be associated with the Runoia camp experience for over a century. In this c. 1914 photograph, co-director Jesse Pound is astride a favorite horse. (Cobb Runoia Collection, BHS.)

This c. 1914 photograph shows Runoia girls taking horse-riding lessons on the Wait Hill farm site. Although the campers were not required to take riding lessons, they were strongly encouraged to do so, and many of them looked forward to the opportunity. (Cobb Runoia Collection, BHS.)

This is a photograph of the Lodge at Camp Arden, a girls' camp that opened in 1914 on the western shore of McGrath Pond in North Belgrade. Arden was a sister camp to Arcadia for boys. The director, Eva M. Teller, was the wife of Camp Arcadia's director, Joseph Teller, and Arden was just a few miles north of Arcadia. Both camps were in operation from 1914 through 1926. (Sturtevant Camps Collection, BHS.)

This is the Shelter, one of the dormitories at Camp Arden. The common English surname Arden may be derived from the Hebrew word for Eden, while Arden Forest is recognizable to anyone familiar with William Shakespeare's comedy *As You Like It*. (Sturtevant Camps Collection, BHS.)

The House in the Woods at Camp Arden is pictured here. Campers were encouraged to participate in acting, music, and various handicrafts at Arden, and they presented plays in this building as part of their summer camp experience. (Sturtevant Camps Collection, BHS.)

This c. 1920 photograph shows the interior of the House in the Woods. Because this building essentially was a theater, its décor tended to change according to which plays were being presented. (Sturtevant Camps Collection, BHS.)

Seen here is the "Studio" building at Camp Arden. Here, the campers had opportunities to experiment with various art and handicraft activities, and at the end of the summer, they could take home various items they made here. The Studio also served as Camp Arden's social hall. (Sturtevant Camps Collection, BHS.)

Camp Somerset was a girls' camp on East Pond in Smithfield. Depending on sources, it opened as early as 1915 or as late as 1921. In its initial years, the girls slept in tents on wooden platforms, as seen in this undated photograph. (Sturtevant Camps Collection, BHS.)

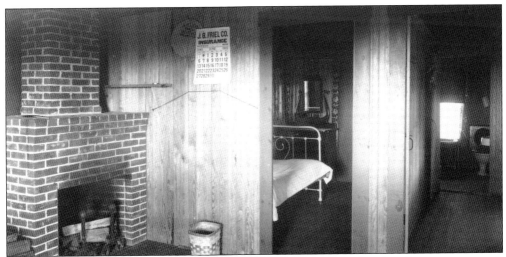

By the late 1920s, cabins such as the one in this photograph had replaced some or even all the original tents at Camp Somerset. The camp closed in the 1980s, but it reopened in 2018. (Sturtevant Camps Collection, BHS.)

This is the Music Room at Camp Somerset. Girls were encouraged to play instruments, and, according to a source who worked in the kitchen from 1939 to 1943, group singing around the campfire or beside the fireplace was typical in the evenings. (Sturtevant Camps Collection, BHS.)

Jo-Lee, a girls' camp located on the southeastern shore of Great Pond just north of Pine Island (North Belgrade), was in operation from 1920 to 1926. Girls slept in the cabins by the lake shore, as seen here. (Sturtevant Camps Collection, BHS.)

This photograph from the early 1920s shows how some Camp Jo-Lee campers decorated their dorm-like cabin. It is likely that such décor was typical at Jo-Lee, as teenage girls (and boys) from upper-class families were fascinated with colleges in this era. (Sturtevant Camps Collection, BHS.)

This group photograph from the early 1920s shows Jo-Lee campers with their camp director in front of the administration building/dining hall. (Sturtevant Camps Collection, BHS.)

This is the social hall at Birch Crest girls' camp on East Pond in Oakland. Birch Crest was a sister camp to Cedar Crest boys' camp. The camps were under the direction of Joseph (Cedar Crest) and Rose Gorfinkle (Birch Crest) and operated from 1926 to 1944. (Sturtevant Camps Collection, BHS.)

SWIMMING AND BOATING FROM CAMP LOWN, OAKLAND, MAINE   K87

Camp Lown (1945–1968) was the first coed youth camp in the Belgrade Lakes region. Its mission was to provide Jewish youth with a summer camp experience steeped in Jewish religious values, culinary traditions, and the observance of prescribed prayers. (Sturtevant Camps Collection, BHS.)

Camp Runoia's move from its cramped location on Salmon Lake to a much larger property on Great Pond included many benefits, such as a secluded sandy beach, where these campers are testing their swimming skills in their 1915 bathing suits. (Cobb Runoia Collection, BHS.)

Runoia's new site also had ample space for horse-riding trails. The campers in this photograph are testing their skills with co-director Jesse Pound (second from left) and a riding instructor (far left). (Cobb Runoia Collection, BHS.)

Runoia employed numerous summer workers to keep the camp operating smoothly. This 1915 photograph shows an unidentified kitchen helper who may have worked for one of the camp directors in the fall, winter, and spring and was recruited to come work at their Maine camp in the summer. (Cobb Runoia Collection, BHS.)

In 1915, Camp Runoia girls pose for a group photograph before departing for home at the end of the summer. (Cobb Runoia Collection, BHS.)

Constance Dowd is pictured in this c. 1919 image at the end of her last year as a camper. She returned as a counselor for several summers while she was in college and graduate school, and subsequently became the assistant director. She loved Runoia and oversaw its development over many years. (Cobb Runoia Collection, BHS.)

Seven

CONTINUITY AND CHANGE IN THE 21ST CENTURY

A loon with chicks swims on upper Long Pond in Rome in 2020. The loon, with its unique, plaintive call, has been the iconic waterbird on all seven of the Belgrade lakes since the beginning of tourism in the 1870s. The loon spends nine months on the Atlantic coast, but mature birds come to Maine's freshwater lakes every summer to mate and raise their chicks. While the loon remains an endearing symbol of the region, since the 1950s, loons, like the Belgrade lakes overall, have been struggling with multiple environmental challenges. Organizations like the older Belgrade Lakes Association and the newer 7 Lakes Alliance are working to keep the lakes healthy for both tourists and wildlife. (Craig Killingbeck.)

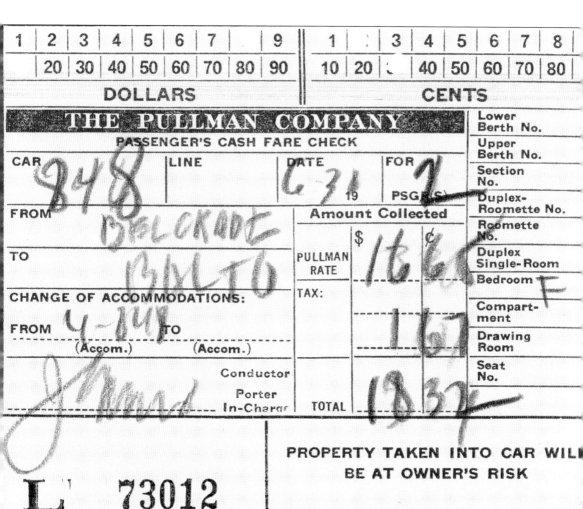

1	2	3	4	5	6	7		9		1		3	4	5	6	7	8
	20	30	40	50	60	70	80	90		10	20		40	50	60	70	80

DOLLARS **CENTS**

THE PULLMAN COMPANY

PASSENGER'S CASH FARE CHECK

| | | | | Lower Berth No. |
| CAR *848* | LINE | DATE *6 31* 19 | FOR *1* PSG(S) | Upper Berth No. |

FROM *BELGRADE*

TO *BALTO*

	Amount Collected	
	$	¢
PULLMAN RATE	*16 6*	
TAX:	*1 67*	

Section No.

Duplex-Roomette No.

Roomette No.

Duplex Single-Room

Bedroom *F*

Compartment

Drawing Room

Seat No.

CHANGE OF ACCOMMODATIONS:

FROM *4-141* TO

(Accom.)   (Accom.)

Conductor

Porter
In-Charge

TOTAL *18 32*

PROPERTY TAKEN INTO CAR WILL BE AT OWNER'S RISK

L 73012

Seen here is one of the last train tickets issued at Belgrade Depot. Central Maine Railroad discontinued passenger service to both Belgrade train stations in 1954. It was a serious blow to the region's tourist industry, especially for the Belgrade and other hotels. (Pauline Plourde Collection, BHS.)

After the end of passenger rail service, the Belgrade Christian Fellowship purchased the North Belgrade train station, moved it to the head of Station Road at Route 11 (Oakland Road), and converted it into this nondenominational church, primarily by the addition of the steeple and minor interior renovations. (Old House Survey, BHS.)

The new brick Central School in Belgrade Depot is seen here when it was completed in November 1943 after a fire nine months earlier destroyed the original 1924 wooden school. Like its predecessor, the high school occupied the upper floor, while "the grades" were on the first floor. Belgrade High School closed in 1968; since then, Belgrade students attend high school in Oakland. (Naurine Kelly Lord Collection, BHS.)

Ed Taylor inspects apples loaded in barrels for transport to nearby Belgrade Depot around 1942. Taylor owned the general store in the large building behind him. Most of Belgrade's apple trees were killed in the historic deep freeze of winter 1934, but a few orchards survived or were replanted. (Pauline Plourde Collection, BHS.)

Oliver Yeaton (left) and Clifton "Skip" Hammond are pictured in the summer of 1944. They founded the HandY Pulp Co. while they were still students at Belgrade High School. After World War II, Hammond founded the Hammond Lumber Company, which gradually grew to become Maine's leading building supply retailer, with branch stores and showrooms throughout the state. (David Yeaton Collection, BHS.)

This is the Belgrade High School class of 1945 graduation photograph. Clifton Hammond, standing at center, is the only boy because the others had left to join the armed forces during the winter and spring. Standing on the left is Lydia Farnham Johnson, who later would establish the Brass Knocker gift shop, a legendary Belgrade Lakes village store where tourists found the perfect gift for 60 years. (Phronie Guptill Hammond Collection, BHS.)

The Brass Knocker gift shop is seen here in the early 1950s. It was located in the living room (front left) of the Walter and Lydia Johnson home on Route 27/Main Street, as visitors entered Belgrade Lakes village driving north on Route 27. Walter Johnson was a son of early Belgrade lakes guide Ernest Johnson. (Carol Johnson Collection, BHS.)

The Brass Knocker gift shop is pictured around 1995 in its new home that Walter Johnson built to the left of the Johnson house. The store closed after Lydia Johnson passed away in October 2011, six weeks before her 93rd birthday. A different but equally famous shop subsequently opened here: the Hello, Good Pie bakery. (Carol Johnson Collection, BHS.)

The old Washington Grammar School in North Belgrade near the corner of Route 8 and Horse Point Road was vacant for several years but now is the North Belgrade Community Center and home to the Belgrade-Rome Food Pantry, where volunteers pack up essential food items each week for needy families, including many elderly residents. (Sturtevant Collection, BHS.)

The "new" Belgrade Lakes grammar school on School Street operated from 1929 to 1968. It was renovated during the early 1970s into the Belgrade Regional Health Center (BHRC), with a large added room in the rear. After 30 years, the BHRC had outgrown its home, and following a successful fundraising effort, it moved in 2009 to a much larger facility on Route 27 in Belgrade. (BHRC.)

After the old Belgrade Lakes grammar school closed in June 1929, the new Veterans of World War I organization purchased and renovated it, lifting the roof to add a second story, cleaning out the privies, and adding a new room to the rear. The finished project opened as the American Legion Hall in 1932. (Sturtevant Collection, BHS.)

Aging membership and lack of interest among younger veterans in joining during the post-Vietnam era forced the VFW to sell its building to private owners in the 1980s. By 2013, Dockside Physical Therapy and a printing shop occupied the building. (BHS.)

Janet George poses for a c. 1946 photograph by a road sign on the way to Bang's Beach, a popular swimming park from the 1940s to the 1960s. It was located on Lake Messalonskee in Sidney. (Janet George Collection, BHS.)

Three friends enjoy Bang's Beach in the late 1940s. Patrons arrived by private car, paid an entrance fee based on the number of persons per car, parked in the designated parking area, enjoyed the beach all day, and could buy drinks and snacks at the concession stand. It was a lake version of the beaches on the ocean. (Janet George Collection, BHS.)

Marie Nagem arrives at the Lakeshore in May 1958 to open it for the summer season. She and her husband, Michael, bought Ervin Bean's house and store after he died in 1940 and bought the Lakeshore in 1947. The children in Belgrade Lakes village affectionately called her "Ma Nagem" because she dished out generous scoops of ice cream for them at the soda fountain in Bean's renamed Nagem's store. (Janet George Collection, BHS.)

The burning of the Belgrade Hotel and other changes negatively impacted old-fashioned hotels like the Lakeshore, which closed in 1962. Private interests purchased the property and demolished all the buildings except the new lobby, which became a private camp. This 1969 photograph shows the empty lot where the main four-story building with the dining room overlooking Long Lake had been; the ell connecting it to the lobby remained to become a kitchen. (Author's collection.)

Frank Farnham drives a tractor on his farm around the early 1950s. Much of his produce was sold at Farnham's Market on Route 27, south of Belgrade Depot. For 40-plus years, the market was a must-stop for summer camp owners who loved its corn, peas, and other produce. (Farnham Collection, BHS.)

This is a 1958 photograph of Day's Store in Belgrade Lakes village. A store has been at this location since the early 19th century. The current structure was rebuilt by David Golder and his sons Henry and Thomas in the early 1880s. The interior has undergone many modifications since 1945. The Day family has owned the store since 1958. (Pauline Plourde Collection, BHS.)

Ed Megill sold the Locusts House to the Povandie family in 1965. They undertook extensive renovations and then reopened it as the Village Inn, with recipes such as slow-roasted duck, that have become legendary. Although the ownership has changed over the years, it still serves Priscilla Povandie's slow-roasted duck, as well as many creative nouvelle cuisine dishes. (Village Inn Collection, BHS.)

The increasing number of Catholics among the early tourists were able to hold services in a Belgrade Hotel room until 1913, when St. Helena's Catholic Church was built on East Road (now Route 27), opposite the hotel's seventh fairway. The church, open only in the summers, celebrated its 100th anniversary in 2013. (Alter Family Collection, BHS.)

A great blue heron spreads its wings on a boulder near the lakeshore in the summer of 2020. These large birds come to the Belgrade lakes in the summers to feed on small fish, mate, and raise chicks. Like loons, both parents care for the chicks. Blue herons may fly as far as Florida for the winter. (Craig Killingbeck.)

Pictured is a traditional early 20th-century boathouse on Mill Stream in Rome. It has been illegal to build boathouses on the lakeshore since the 1970s, but those built earlier, like this one, are permitted to remain, although they cannot be enlarged. (Johnson-Mathias Boat Collection, BHS.)

Although Oakland is known for its summer camps, it also was an important small manufacturing center, initially specializing in axes and scythes, and later, factories making wood products and woolen textiles. The Cascade Woolen Mill, seen here, opened on Messalonskee Stream in 1882 and operated for just over 100 years. (Merrow Collection, BHS.)

Gould Rogers addresses the Belgrade town meeting in March 1972. As a young man and station master at Belgrade Depot, he met, fell in love with, and married Alta Poland, the first telegraph operator at the Belgrade Hotel. Rogers and his wife actively participated in the civic and social organizations of Belgrade for more than 50 years. (Pauline Plourde Collection, BHS.)

The Grange in Belgrade Depot was one of the civic organizations in which Gould and Alta Rogers participated. As the number of farming families decreased after 1960, the Grange gradually became less active, and the building was sold in the late 20th century. (Old House Survey, BHS.)

This 2020 photograph shows a sailboat moored offshore on Long Pond, near the Belgrade-Rome water boundary. Although sailboats are common on Great Pond, the largest of the seven Belgrade lakes, they also can be seen on Long Pond and the other lakes in the summer. (Craig Killingbeck.)

This is a rare view of a summer camp in winter. This camp is on Beaver Cove, the northernmost part of Upper Long Pond, which is in Rome. It seems the proprietors did not get their summer furniture stowed before the first snow arrived. (Craig Killingbeck.)

A lone fisherman casts near the dam where Mill Stream empties into Long Pond. Fishing has remained the primary sport of the lakes for 150 years. The hills of Rome visible in the background are Blueberry Hill on the left and Round Top on the right. (Craig Killingbeck.)

124

Main Street in Belgrade Lakes village is pictured in 2019 as Maine's Department of Transportation completes its year-long reconstruction of Route 27/Main Street. Note the new brick sidewalks and streetlights paid for by the private, nonprofit Friends of the Village, a new organization that continues a century-long tradition of civic engagement in the region. (Craig Killingbeck.)

This 1928 Model A Ford was purchased two decades ago by its Belgrade owner because it reminded him of his grandfather's 1928 Ford truck and his father's Model A coupe. It is a star in the annual Fourth of July parade that begins on Route 27, where summer camps line the Rome shore of Long Pond and slowly proceed south to the bridge at the dam, into Belgrade Lakes village, and down Main Street. (Rodney Johnson.)

BIBLIOGRAPHY

Brown, H. Leslie. "The History of Belgrade Lakes." Unpublished, 1976.

Deyo, Simeon L., and Henry D. Kingsbury. *Illustrated History of Kennebec County, Maine: 1625–1799–1892.* Tucson, AZ: W.C. Cox & Co., 1974.

Guptill, R.A., C.F. Nye, and H.P. Plourde. *Past and present: Pictures and people of Belgrade, Maine, 1774–1976.* Belgrade, ME: Heritage Committee of Belgrade Bicentennial Observance, 1976.

Johnson, Rodney. *The Whole Kit and Caboodle: Tales from the Luckiest Boy.* Self-published, 2021.

Oakland Historical Society. *Oakland.* Charleston, SC: Arcadia Publishing, 2004.

Penney, John William, and Minnie Penney. *Eighty-Eight Years on a Maine Farm.* Camden, ME: Down East Books, 2021.

Sweet, Melissa. *Some Writer!: The Story of E.B. White.* New York, NY: Houghton, Mifflin, Harcourt, 2016.

White, E.B. *Essays of E.B. White.* New York, NY: Harper Perennial Modern Classics, 1999.

White, E.B., Dorothy Lobrano Guth, and Martha White. *Letters of E.B. White.* New York, NY: Harper Perennial, 2007.

Wilson, Donald A. *Maine Lodges and Sporting Camps.* Charleston, SC: Arcadia Publishing, 2005.

Yeaton, Carl, Ralph Endicott, and Myron Buchak. *Town of Belgrade, Past and Present, Pictures-Places-People, 1796–1996.* Belgrade, ME: Heritage Committee, 1996.

DISCOVER THOUSANDS OF LOCAL HISTORY BOOKS
FEATURING MILLIONS OF VINTAGE IMAGES

Arcadia Publishing, the leading local history publisher in the United States, is committed to making history accessible and meaningful through publishing books that celebrate and preserve the heritage of America's people and places.

Find more books like this at
www.arcadiapublishing.com

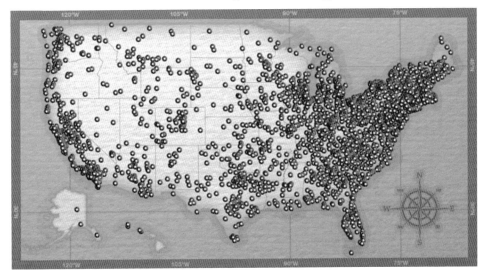

Search for your hometown history, your old stomping grounds, and even your favorite sports team.

Consistent with our mission to preserve history on a local level, this book was printed in South Carolina on American-made paper and manufactured entirely in the United States. Products carrying the accredited Forest Stewardship Council (FSC) label are printed on 100 percent FSC-certified paper.

MADE IN THE

USA